PRESCRIPTION TO FLIP AND WIN IN REAL ESTATE:

AN ETHICAL GUIDE TO REAL ESTATE INVESTING

Laquita Brooks

Cover Design: Ayo
Editor: Tosha Smith Mills
ISBN: 9798324475918

"The best investment on earth is earth." – Louis Rickman

"I view real estate as the most intriguing opportunity that I've seen in my business lifetime." – Richard Rainwater

Table of Contents

Introduction

———◆◇◆———

"Real Estate provides the highest returns, the greatest
values and the least risk." - Armstrong Williams

———◆◇◆———

Most people are slaves to their spending on the wrong things. Because debt is becoming increasingly common, it is now known as the new form of modern-day slavery. Today, over six million credit cards are used in this Country, and one out of every three consumer purchases is made with a credit card. This is shocking. What is also very shocking is that consumers prefer the appearance of wealth over real wealth. Every day, we make financial decisions that choose between our lifestyle today and financial freedom tomorrow.

As a serial entrepreneur who owns several businesses, I am often asked, "Why real estate investing? My answer is always the same, it's the smartest way to financial freedom. According to the New York Federal Reserve, consumer debt was approaching $14 trillion after the third quarter of 2019. There has been consistent growth in four main areas of debt – home, auto, student loans, and credit cards. Whether it's an expensive car loan or designer clothes, you bought with a credit card, an emphasis on lifestyle over financial freedom can lead to life-long financial bondage. When asked the question, "Why real estate?" I must remind myself and so many others, why not real estate? Why not take my money and invest it back into something that builds collateral and generational wealth?

After spending an hour or two reading this book, you will make a conscious decision that one of the best ways to financial freedom and generational wealth is through real estate. It is very easy to understand—no jargon. With some help and hard work, you can create a legacy to pass down to the next generation. Thank you for accepting the prescription for my book and getting it filled.

Laquita Brooks

THE JOURNEY

The journey started approximately twenty-five years ago. Being an entrepreneur at a very young age, I wanted to know what millionaires were doing to become billionaires, and two things came to mind: purchasing real estate and investing in the stock market.

While viewing homes with my husband, I became more interested in what the realtor did than in purchasing my first home. I was always interested in the home's aesthetics, watching home improvement shows and flipping through magazines, but more than anything, listening to my realtor put an exciting twist on real estate investing. I just had to get into real estate.

After purchasing my first property to flip, I knew that this was not only my passion and purpose, but real estate was lucrative and could potentially be a modest goal to make extra money on top of my other ventures. I have now grown my real estate portfolio extensively by investing in underpriced homes in need of a little love, renovating them as inexpensively as possible, and then reselling them for a profit.

I now teach others how to pivot in real estate and bring real HGTV to life.

HOW IT WORKS

Flipping houses takes work. First, you need to understand the flipping method and what it means. Flipping is also known as wholesale real estate investing. It is when an investor purchases a property not to live in but intends to fix it up and sell it for profit. The first rule is to buy low and sell high. The goal is to complete the transaction as quickly as possible to limit the time your capital is at risk.

Buy, fix up, sell, and repeat. The longer you hold on to the property, the more money it costs you (the investor). Until that property is sold, you are paying the mortgage (unless you buy with cash), utilities, insurance, and any other costs associated with being a homeowner.

Real estate investing and flipping are very rewarding. If you think you will get rich by flipping a house, close this book and rethink your objectives because you will not succeed. This endeavor requires money, planning, patience, skills, and effort. Real Estate can be expensive and is a time-consuming venture.

If I can give you any advice, that would be to limit your financial risk. Do not pay too much for a property without knowing its worth. Do your homework before purchasing that property by knowing how much the necessary repairs and upgrades will cost you. After figuring out the critical pieces of the amount it will cost you, you will determine an ideal purchase price.

KNOW THE AREA

NEIGHBORHOOD ANALYSIS

K Nowing the area where you are seeking to purchase a property is very important. Whether it is a "cash cow" rental property that generates a monthly cash flow or a property that you want to buy, fix up, and resell, known as a "flip," analyzing that neighborhood is very important. Each of the above properties has one thing in common, and that is that the neighborhood analysis would meet or exceed the buyer's investment objectives.

The most important piece about real estate investing is location. What is a neighborhood analysis? The neighborhood analysis will help you reveal how attractive the property you are looking for will be in the forthcoming months or years. For example, if the surrounding houses are blighted and uncared for, you can put a million dollars into the home and may not be able to sell it. Even if the market is strong in that area, buying a property in the wrong place can decrease mark value over time.

If you see a large number of "For Rent" or "For Sale" signs, that is an indication that the area is not as good as it may seem, even when the price is low. An area that would be a great investment show has low vacancies and a high level of demand instead of vacant properties everywhere.

FINANCING IN PLACE

CASH IS KING

Purchasing a property with cash when you are flipping is one of the most brilliant things you can do. There are several reasons why. One of those reasons is that it eliminates the need to pay interest on a loan and any closing costs associated with buying that home. There are no mortgage origination, appraisal, or other fees lenders charge to assess buyers. Paying cash for a property can also mean obtaining that property at a much lower rate, which can potentially come with many discounts. You do not have to wait for an inspection, appraisal, or underwriting.

Another reason is that it is attractive to the seller. In the competitive market we are currently in, the seller is likely to take that cash offer over a buyer who must obtain a mortgage because it is faster and has fewer risks. The buyer can avoid backing out due to financing being denied or negotiating closing costs. It is usually a simple transaction between the buyer and seller and can close much faster.

Cash flow is king in real estate investing because it means immediate cash flow, limited contingencies, less hassle and fees, faster closing, and potential savings.

FINDING YOUR PROPERTY

WAYS TO FIND PROPERTY

Your biggest question you may have will be, "How do I find these houses to flip?" This question has many answers, which can sometimes be a challenge. Let me help you out just a little.

1. Real Estate Agent: Hire an agent who understands the business of real estate investing and flipping properties. Many real estate agents are knowledgeable about selling homes but do not possess investment strategies or experience flipping houses.

2. Find your target market: Find a great home that offers a great deal and needs renovation, which you can sell for above market value.

3. Auctions: When a lender forecloses on a home, the home is usually auctioned off. You can typically find these auctions online. The listing will include the time and date of the auction. Make sure you bring cash.

4. Look for REO Homes: If the home is not sold at an auction, it becomes a real-estate owned (REO) property. This means, the property reverts to the lender. The repairs on these properties are usually extensive.

5. Short Sales: This means the home is sold to a buyer less than the mortgage balance. The repairs may be substantial, but a short sale can be a solid purchase for investors.

6. Public Records: Go to the courts and find properties that owners may owe substantial taxes on and send that homeowner a letter explaining your interest in your home. Finding homes like this holds value for investors.

7. Online: Sites like Zillow Foreclosure Center, FlipScout foreclosures.com and many more can also be online resources.

Knowing the area is intimate knowledge that cannot be replaced, but also remember that buying local in your region is only sometimes the way to go. House flipping is prolific in Georgia, Tennessee, North Carolina, New York, Texas, Virginia, Florida, Illinois, Ohio, and Pennsylvania.

BUILDING A TEAM

THE VALUE OF YOUR TEAM

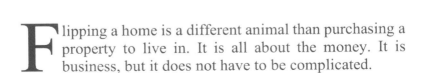

F lipping a home is a different animal than purchasing a property to live in. It is all about the money. It is business, but it does not have to be complicated.

Someone investing in real estate and flipping houses constantly needs a solid team. The number one rule in business is "You are only as good as the team you build." You cannot make money hand over fist without a good team behind you, and all team members shall match your level of commitment. Let us discuss the team.

1. Real Estate Attorney: Hire an attorney who knows real estate law.

2. Real Estate Agent: Find a real estate agent who knows the flipping game. The agent will analyze the market and recommend competitive pricing that will attract buyers.

3. Certified Public Accountant: Find a good accountant familiar with U.S. Tax laws for house-flipping.

4. Insurance Agent: Your insurance agent advises you on insuring different types of properties.

5. Contractors: Contractors can make or break you. You must find contractors that you trust; that will not nickel and dime your entire flipping process and will work within your budget. A general contractor will run the entire project and is responsible for hiring plumbers, electricians, and carpenters.

6. Lenders: If you are not buying the property with cash, as I suggest, make sure you have a great source of funding. Your financing partner is probably the most important person on the team. No cash, no deal. One of the most popular ways for flipping houses is a hard money loan. Hard money lenders are quick to act and have lots of flexibility in their underwriting process.

Remember that no team is perfect, but if you find a good team, and if it is done correctly, they will be your most valuable asset from property to profit. Do not have a problem modifying your team on a deal-to-deal basis. Your success depends on knowing who you work most efficiently with and who can help you bring the highest return on investments for your flip.

ARV

THE 70% RULE

ARV stands for after repair value and is one of the most important terms to know when investing in real estate; ARV is commonly used in house flipping, a short-term real estate investment strategy in which a person buys a "fixer-upper" property, renovates it and sells it for a profit. The after-repair value is the property's value after being improved and renovated. It is used with flippers/rehabbers who flip homes and with any real estate investment in which renovations or improvements to the property would add value. ARV is determined by looking at comparable properties in the recently sold area.

The ARV is commonly used in the house-flipping business. It considers the value of the final renovated property and determines how much to invest in the property you are looking to purchase.

The rule of thumb is that real estate investors should make a 30% return on their investment (ROI). This is also known as the 70% rule. The 70% rule says that an investor should spend no more than 70% of a property's ARV on it. This includes the price you pay for the property and any estimated repair costs.

Example of the 70% Rule

If you estimate a property's ARV will be $300,000.00, you should spend no more than $210,000.00. If the property is estimated to need $50,000.00 in repairs, your purchase price should be no more than $160,000.00.

Experienced investors will always get into a deal with an expected profit in mind. If you are expecting a profit of at least $60,000.00, you would have to start with the $300,000.00 ARV, subtract the total expenses of $91,000.00, and then subtract your minimum acceptable profit of $60,000.00 to reach a maximum offer price of $149,000.00.

If you had only used the 70% rule, you would have paid $11,000.00 more than you should have for this property.

Understanding this is key as it is fundamental in determining whether you will make or lose money. You cannot and will only be successful if you know the ARV rule.

For example, you purchased a property with a current value of $150,000, and you plan to invest $30,000 in renovations and improvements – using the above formula to calculate ARV as follows:

ARV = Property's Current Value + Value of Renovation

$$\$180,000\ ARV = \$150,000 + \$30,000$$

70% RULE

$$\$150,000\ ARV$$
$$X\quad 70\%$$
$$\overline{\$105,000}$$
$$-\ \$25,000\ REPAIRS$$
$$\overline{\$80,000}$$

Let me quickly define some important variables before we get too far ahead of ourselves:

- *After Repair Value (ARV)* – what the house will l be worth once it is renovated.

- *Title Closing Costs on Purchase* – all fees charged by the title company/closing attorney/escrow company to handle the purchase transaction.

- *Loan Closing Costs* – all fees and points charged by the lender to fund the deal.

- *Loan Holding Costs* – loan payments per lender's terms.

- *Carrying Costs* – property taxes, builder's risk insurance, electricity, water, sewer, trash, HOA dues, any other ongoing costs (based on the length of the project.

- ***Title Closings Costs on Sale*** – all fees charged by the title company/closing attorney/escrow company to handle the sale transaction.

- ***Real Estate Agent Commission*** – on the sale, this varies and is not set in stone; this is one of the questions that you must ask your agent.

- ***Net Profit*** - what goes into your pocket after the sale once all expenses are accounted for.

In the 70% Rule, that 30% margin (the difference between 100% and 70%), is intended to cover all those factors above including title closing costs on the purchase, lender points and fees, loan payments, carrying costs, title closing costs on the sale, real estate agent commissions, and a profit.

CONCLUSION

As a woman who has flipped many properties in a male-dominated industry, my empowerment has always been to teach as many people as I can about real estate investing. The advice that I have shared with you was limited and was only a small dose of the actual prescription,

Buying my first piece of property was the most important decision ever because it got me in the game. Real estate investing is not only commonplace but also never-ending because of its demand. Most billionaires who have invested in real estate will tell you that they have built wealth and a comfortable lifestyle for their family, mostly through necessity—not by design. Real estate is becoming more and more popular not by the day but by the moment; it is versatility that makes it broadly appealing.

This mini book is only the catalyst for what else there is to learn—more than I can write, but much more to teach in a masterclass setting. I am a perfectionist who has mastered real estate investing and would love to assist you in mastering it as well.

ABOUT THE AUTHOR

Laquita Brooks, a serial entrepreneur with over twenty years of combined knowledge in business coaching, motivation, and real estate investing, aims to continue transforming lives across the nation by offering simple and direct solutions to some of life's most challenging issues.

Mrs. Brooks is also a philanthropist, generational leader, motivational speaker, and success coach seen on many platforms and publications, including Ebony, Essence, IHeart, and many more. Through her daily broadcasts on social media, Laquita educates her audience on how to push through their deepest desires and begin to thrive in their purpose to be the next millionaire in the making. Her daily thought videos will motivate you to discover and live your dreams out loud that bring you to your destiny.

CONNECT WITH
LAQUITA BROOKS

@mrsbusinesswoman

https://www.facebook.com/laquitabrooks.com

https://www.linkedin.com/in/laquitabrooks-
themotivationalmaven/

www.laquitabrooks.com

Email: nolaempowerment@gmail.com

Made in the USA
Columbia, SC
16 July 2024

38434776R00017